OXFORD
UNIVERSITY PRESS

Great Clarendon Street, Oxford, OX2 6DP,
United Kingdom

Oxford University Press is a department of the
University of Oxford. It furthers the University's
objective of excellence in research, scholarship,
and education by publishing worldwide. Oxford is
a registered trade mark of Oxford University Press in
the UK and in certain other countries

Text © Oxford University Press 2024

Illustrations © Wenke Kramp 2024

The moral rights of the author have been asserted

First Edition published in 2024

All rights reserved. No part of this publication may
be reproduced, stored in a retrieval system, or
transmitted, in any form or by any means, without the
prior permission in writing of Oxford University Press,
or as expressly permitted by law, by licence or under
terms agreed with the appropriate reprographics
rights organization. Enquiries concerning
reproduction outside the scope of the above should
be sent to the Rights Department, Oxford University
Press, at the address above.

You must not circulate this work in any other form and
you must impose this same condition on any acquirer

British Library Cataloguing in Publication Data

Data available

ISBN: 978-1-382-04354-0

10 9 8 7 6 5 4 3 2 1

The manufacturing process conforms to the
environmental regulations of the country of origin.

Printed in China by Golden Cup

Acknowledgements

How to be Friends with an Ostrich and *An Unlikely
Friendship* written by Rob Alcraft

Content on pages 7, 64, 66 and 70 written by
Suzy Ditchburn

Illustrated by Wenke Kramp

Author photo courtesy of Rob Alcraft

The publisher and author would like to thank the
following for permission to use photographs and
other copyright material:

Cover: Juice Team / Shutterstock. Photos: p2,
46(b): Chelsea Sampson / Shutterstock; p30,
31: Moonstone Images / iStock / Getty Images
Plus; p4(m), 34(inset), 37, 62(lt), 70(l): Andrea
Izzotti / Shutterstock; p4(b), 23(t): GoodFocused
/ Shutterstock; p5(t), 22(t), 60(r): Imran Khan's
Photography / Shutterstock; p5 (ml + mr), 28, 47,
60(l), 61(l), 68: aaltair / Shutterstock; p10, 11(bkg):
ArCaLu / Shutterstock; p10, 11(inset), 63(l): Juice
Team / Shutterstock; p12: VladKK / Shutterstock;
p13: Artush / Shutterstock; p20: AB Photographie
/ Shutterstock; p21: Gelpi / Shutterstock; p22(bl),
62(l): Aneta Jungerova / Shutterstock; p22(br),
63(r): SasaStock / Shutterstock; p23(b), 61(r): Odua
Images / Shutterstock; p26, 27, 59: cbimages /
Alamy Stock Photo; p33, 67, 69: FLPA / Alamy Stock
Photo; p34, 35, 70(r): Stefan Pircher / Shutterstock;
p36, 58: By Fiona Ayerst / Shutterstock; p38: Phil
Degginger / Alamy Stock Photo; p40, 41: Danita
Delimont / Shutterstock; p42: Roma Likhvan /
Shutterstock; p44: Sergey Lavrentev / Shutterstock;
p45: Smeerjewegproducties / Shutterstock; p46(t):
Martin Pelanek / Shutterstock; p48, 49: Rich Carey /
Shutterstock; p51: Joe Belanger / Shutterstock; p56:
Thinkstock / Stockbyte / Getty Images.

Every effort has been made to contact copyright
holders of material reproduced in this book. Any
omissions will be rectified in subsequent printings if
notice is given to the publisher.

How to be Friends with an Ostrich

Written by Rob Alcraft
Illustrated by Wenke Kramp

OXFORD
UNIVERSITY PRESS

Have a go!

ei as in ceiling

i as in police

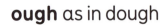

ough as in dough

Read this book if ... you want to learn

INCREDIBLE FACTS

about

STRANGE ANIMAL FRIENDSHIPS!

STOP AND THINK

In this book, you will find out all about animals that help each other to survive.

Do you know any animals that help each other?

Contents

Let's be friends 10

Learn to share 18

Be useful 28

Be special 38

Team up 48

Friends forever! 58

Glossary 60

Index 62

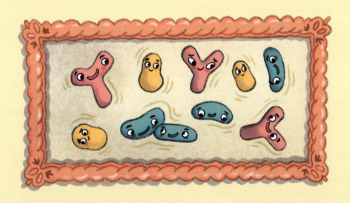

Let's be friends

Good news!

You don't need a very **long** neck to be friends with an ostrich.

YOU COULD BE STRIPY.

Ostriches and zebras like hanging out. Ostriches have **super** eyesight and zebras have a **great** sense of smell. Together they are more likely to avoid nasty surprises – like being **eaten**.

keeps a look out

14

Ostriches and zebras like hanging out. Ostriches have **super** eyesight and zebras have a **great** sense of smell. Together they are more likely to avoid nasty surprises – like being **eaten**.

sniffs out danger

This friendship works because it helps **both** animals. The world is full of friendships like this.

Choose your friends!

Can you pair these **unlikely friends?**

Find out which creatures get along …

Learn to share!

Lots of **odd** pairs of creatures live together. We are one of them!

Dogs started out **WILD**. At least 12000 years ago, they began to be friends with humans.
Since then, we've bred them to be *gentler*. There are now lots of kinds of friendly dogs!

HUMANS LOOK AFTER DOGS.

21

Dogs help us in lots of ways!

I'm good with sheep.

I can locate things.

I'll help you get about safely.

I'm really good company!

I can pull a sledge.

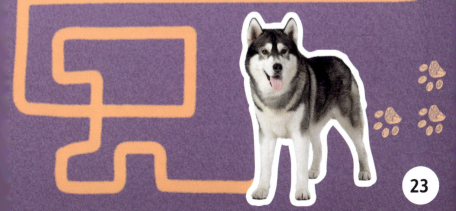

Do you think that these two would be good together?

can't spot danger

snapper shrimp

ace at digging **burrows**

The snapper shrimp lets the goby fish share its burrow. The goby fish keeps watch when they go outside.

Pst! You want to be friends?

Be useful

Even if you're **small**, you can have ***MONSTER-SIZED*** friends. Just make sure you're useful! Otherwise, you might end up as a **snack**.

Hummm!

This little humming frog has the ***SCARIEST*** friend ever.

Yikes!

Tarantulas **paralyse** animals they want to eat. First they **bite** them. Then they **suck up** their insides like a milkshake.

The tarantula and frog snuggle up in the **same** burrow. It's **amazing!** Each is useful to the other.

needs help keeping her eggs safe from ants

enormous and scary looking

tarantula

The frog keeps the tarantula's eggs safe from **munching** ants. In return, the tarantula protects the frog from danger.

win-win!

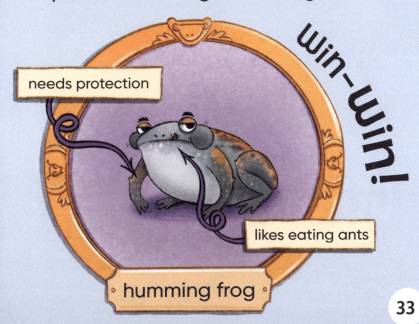

needs protection

likes eating ants

humming frog

Now it's **your** turn. You are a snack-sized fish about to meet a **SHARK**. How can you be useful?

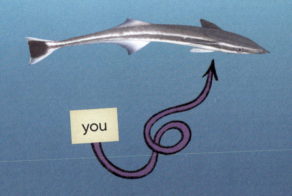

you

QUICK, THINK!

BE USEFUL ... OR BE EATEN!

That's it!

Although sharks have big teeth, they **don't** have arms. They can't **scratch** annoying itches or care for their skin. That's where **you** come in. You can keep the shark clean!

These remora fish eat dead skin off the shark. The shark receives a good old clean. The remora fish get protection and a tasty snack.

Enormous friends are useful!

Tell someone about one fact you've learned so far.

Be special

Would you grow a **silly** nose for your friends?

The right nose can help you get food. This bat has a **long** nose compared with other bats.

Its nose helps it reach the **nectar** in this flower.

Just like the bat, lots of creatures are friendly with flowering plants. The creatures get **HIGH-ENERGY** nectar. In return, they help plants with **pollination**. Pollination is needed to make new plants.

When creatures feed from a flower, pollen gets **STUCK** to them. They carry the pollen to the next flower.

pollen

The pollen rubs off onto the flower.

The flower is pollinated!

Compare these flower-friendly body parts!

honey possum

hummingbird

Team up

Some friends are so **close**, they live in the **same** body!

These **CORALS** are not just an *ANIMAL* and not just a plant. They're a little bit of **both**!

Each giant **CORAL** is made up of thousands of **tiny** body-sharing teams.

This is pure **teamwork**: **two** kinds of life, sharing one body. Each **one** is needed for the other to stay alive.

We swap and share everything!

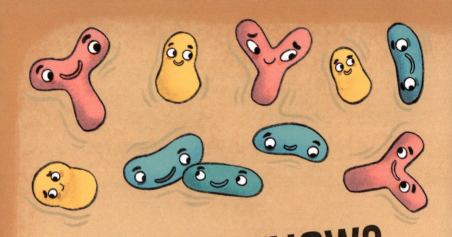

DID YOU KNOW? YOU SHARE YOUR BODY, TOO!

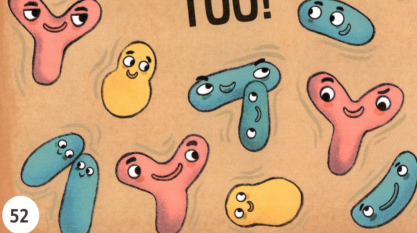

Your body is home to **billions** of **microbes**. They're **tiny** creatures that are too small to see – but they're still your **friends!**

Your **billions** of microbes don't take up much space. They would probably only fill a **little** cup.

Your microbes help you **digest** food.

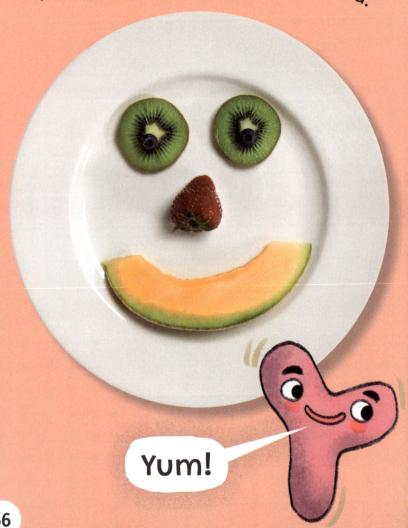

Your friendly microbes give you **vitamins**. They also help you fight germs that cause diseases.

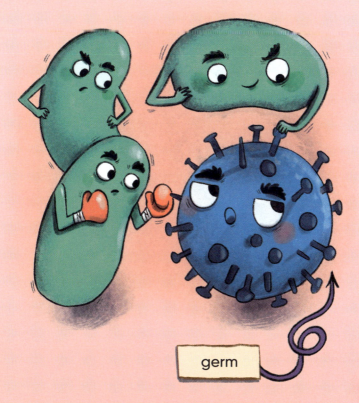

germ

In return, you give them somewhere cosy to live and plenty of food.

57

Friends forever!

Do you have an **enormous** neck? A **long** nose? It could be an opportunity to make friends. Most creatures in the world rely on teamwork to stay alive.

Glossary

burrows: holes dug by animals to live in

digest: to soften and change food in the stomach and other organs, so that the body can absorb it

microbes: tiny creatures that can only be seen with a microscope

nectar: a sweet liquid collected by animals from flowers

paralyse: to make something unable to move

pollen: a yellow powder found inside flowers, containing seeds

pollination: putting pollen into a flower or plant so it can make new plants

vitamins: things which are present in some foods which you need to stay healthy

Index

bat	38–41
coral	48–51
dog	19–23
goby fish	25–27
human	18, 20–21
humming frog	28, 32–33
microbes	52–57

ostrich 10–11, 13–15

pollination 42–45

remora fish 34–37

shark 34–37

snapper shrimp 24, 26–27

tarantula 30–33

zebra 12–13, 15

Look back

1. Why do animals pair up together?
2. How do sharks keep clean without hands?
3. Which pairing do you find the most interesting? Why?

Ha! Ha!

What do you call a friendly dog?

Man's best fur-end.

Read out loud

On the next page, there is a conversation between a tarantula and a humming frog. They are discussing how they can help each other.

Find a friend and read together. Think about what sort of voice each animal would have. Practise their voices. If you'd like to, perform to your class.

conversation

An Unlikely Friendship

Oh tarantula,
I love your hairy legs!
You're so big and scary,
will you keep me safe?
I know my humming is annoying,
but let's be friends, let's share.

You're quite right, frog!
Your humming hurts my head.

But see these pesky ants?
They want my eggs, my babies!

Eat the ants and it's a deal:
we'll be friends, we'll share.

Read it again

1. Read the conversation again, adding more feeling to your voice to reflect the animals and what is being said.

2. Write a conversation between two other animals. What might they say to each other?

Think about what each animal can offer the other and how they might persuade each other to help.